Courage

Joy

Lee Gatiss

Courage, Persistence, Joy
by Lee Gatiss
© Church Society 2024
Church Society
Ground Floor, Centre Block
Hille Business Estate, 132 St Albans Road Watford WD24 4AE, UK
Tel +44 (0)1923 255410
www.churchsociety.org
admin@churchsociety.org
Unless otherwise stated, all Scripture quotations are taken from The Holy Bible, New International Version. Copyright © 1973, 1978, 1984, 2011 by Biblica, Inc. Used by permission. All rights reserved. All rights reserved. Except as may be permitted by the Copyright Act, no part of this publication may be reproduced in any form or by any means without prior permission from the publisher.

Printed in the UK
ISBN: 978-1-7395160-4-8

Contents

Courage 5

Persistence.. 23

Joy 39

Courage

You may know that old joke about the university student who sat down in an exam to find the first question was this: "What is courage?" And apparently they only wrote two words:

"This is."

Then they got up and left the examination room.

I don't know whether that's true or not. But it's a question I've often pondered. What is courage? A good place to find out is the first chapter of Philippians. The Apostle Paul writes:

Paul and Timothy, servants of Christ Jesus,

To all God's holy people in Christ Jesus at Philippi, together with the overseers and deacons:

Grace and peace to you from God our Father and the Lord Jesus Christ.

I thank my God every time I remember you. In all my prayers for all of you, I always pray with joy because of your partnership in the gospel from the first day until now, being confident of this, that he who began a good work in you will carry it on to completion until the day of Christ Jesus.

It is right for me to feel this way about all of you, since I have you in my heart and, whether I am in chains or defending and confirming the gospel, all of you share in God's grace with me. God can testify how I long for all of you with the affection of Christ Jesus.

And this is my prayer: that your love may abound more and more in knowledge and depth of insight, so that you may be able to discern what is best and may be pure and blameless for the day of Christ, filled with the fruit of righteousness that comes through Jesus Christ—to the glory and praise of God.

Now I want you to know, brothers and sisters, that what has happened to me has actually served to advance the gospel. As a result, it has become clear throughout the whole palace guard and to everyone else that I am in chains for Christ. ***And because of my chains, most of the brothers and sisters have become confident in the Lord and dare all the more to proclaim the gospel without fear.***

It is true that some preach Christ out of envy and rivalry, but others out of goodwill. The latter do so out of love, knowing that I am put here for the defence of the gospel. The former preach

Christ out of selfish ambition, not sincerely, supposing that they can stir up trouble for me while I am in chains. But what does it matter? The important thing is that in every way, whether from false motives or true, Christ is preached. And because of this I rejoice.

Yes, and I will continue to rejoice, for I know that through your prayers and God's provision of the Spirit of Jesus Christ what has happened to me will turn out for my deliverance. ***I eagerly expect and hope that I will in no way be ashamed, but will have sufficient courage so that now as always Christ will be exalted in my body, whether by life or by death.*** *For to me, to live is Christ and to die is gain. If I am to go on living in the body, this will mean fruitful labour for me. Yet what shall I choose? I do not know! I am torn between the two: I desire to depart and be with Christ, which is better by far; but it is more necessary for you that I* *remain in the body. Convinced of this, I know that I will remain, and I will continue with all of you for your progress and joy in the faith, so that through my being with you again your boasting in Christ Jesus will abound on account of me.*

Whatever happens, conduct yourselves in a manner worthy of the gospel of Christ. Then, whether I come and see you or only hear about you in my absence, I will know that you stand firm in the one Spirit, striving together as one for the faith of the gospel without being frightened in any way by those who oppose you. This is a sign to them that they will be destroyed, but that you will be saved—and that by God. For it has been granted to you on behalf of Christ not only to believe in him, but also to suffer for him, since you are going through the same struggle you saw I had, and now hear that I still have.

There are lots of things in this chapter. But

I think what we learn about courage here is this: Courage is unashamedly proclaiming the gospel together, whatever the cost.

Confidence in the face of fear

There are two main verses for us to focus on. First, verse 14: "And because of my chains, most of the brothers and sisters have become *confident* in the Lord and *dare* all the more to proclaim the gospel without fear." Paul is in prison because of his open proclamation of the good news of Jesus. But rather than making the Christians around him somewhat wary of speaking out themselves, it has only made them more confident. That word *confident* speaks of assurance in a situation which might normally cause fear or dismay. Their hearts are not cowardly, but convinced.

Indeed, they are *daring*. They dare to double-down on the gospel, and preach it all the more, despite what has happened to Paul. This is the same daring courage that Joseph of Arimathea had when he took a deep breath and went in to ask Pilate for the body of Jesus (Mark 15:43). It may be "fearless", in one way, but that's not because there was nothing to fear. Rather, true courage is facing up to fear. As the philosopher Cicero (106-43 BC) said, "fortitude is deliberate facing of dangers and bearing of toils."[1] Or I think it was President Franklin Delano Roosevelt who once wrote, "Courage is not the absence of fear, but rather the assessment that something else is more important than fear."[2]

For the Christians Paul is talking about here, that important something else was the courageous proclamation of the truth in the face of opposition. And that was part of their partnership with Paul. In verse 5, Paul says he thanks God for that same partnership he has with the Philippians. And in verse 27 he urges them to "Strive *together as one* for the faith of the gospel, without being fright-

---

1 Cicero, *De Inventione*, II.163. Cf. *Rhetorica ad Herennium*, III.3.

2 See Teri Kanefield, *The Making of America*. Franklin D. Roosevelt (New York: Abrams, 2019), chapter 5.

ened in any way by those who oppose you."

While the courage of one can be inspiring and strengthening — whether that's Paul in prison, or a bishop taking an unpopular stand for orthodox faith in General Synod or on a video, or a minister preaching clearly on the hot button issues of the day, or a worker daring to speak up about such things in their day job — courage is something we can also do together.

Fans of the *Lord of the Rings* films may remember Aragorn's speech at the Black Gate, as his fearful army prepared to fight against insurmountable odds to give poor Frodo a chance: "A day may come when the *courage* of men fails. When we forsake our friends and break all bonds of fellowship. But it is not this day." We can't do courage alone — we need each other, those "bonds of fellowship". It damages all of us if we step away and distance ourselves from the battles we all face. It saps our collective courage. Standing together as many of us have done recently on contested issues means more to us as evangelicals than whatever it is that might tempt us to draw back or feel ashamed of those who stand with us.

When Ezra was praying and working for reform and renewal of God's people in the Old Testament, he said, "Because the hand of the LORD my God was on me, *I took courage* and gathered leaders from Israel to go up with me" out of Babylon (Ezra 7:28). Reformation and renewal of the church is something which happens when leaders gather to take counsel together, and have the courage to then go on together (see also Malachi 3:16).

Boldness in the face of struggles

The second verse which is especially relevant in Philippians 1, is verse 20. Paul is grateful for their prayers for him while he is suffering. And he writes, "I eagerly expect and hope that I will in no way be *ashamed*, but will have sufficient *courage* so that now as always Christ will be exalted in my body, whether by life or by death."

Underlying this is a different Greek word for courage. Here it's more about boldness, freedom to speak, in what might be intimidating circumstances. Just as Paul writes elsewhere of having *freedom and confidence* to approach God, in Christ and through faith in him (Ephesians 3:12), here Paul says he hopes for unashamed, confident courage to say what needs to be said. Whether he lives or dies because of it.

And again, this is something shared with the Philippians. Verse 29 says "For it has been granted to *you* on behalf of Christ not only to believe in him, but also to suffer for him." They have the same struggle, and the same need for courage as Paul.

So, Philippians 1 gives us a picture of courage which is very different from that of the world around us. In our culture, courage is often simply *self*-confidence. *Self*-assurance. The courage to be me.

But Philippians 1 tells us that courage is unashamedly proclaiming the gospel together, whatever the cost. And courage begets courage. Hearing survivors of abuse talk bravely about the things they suffered puts courage into others who were similarly abused, as we have seen with some recent scandals. Watching brothers and sisters who experience same-sex attraction remain openly committed to the church's traditional teaching about this, despite the pressures they face to abandon it, puts courage into others to stick their necks out too. Seeing Paul in prison for his faith, facing frightening opposition and proclaiming the gospel anyway – this put steel in the backbones of the Christians around him. God has not given us a spirit of timidity, but a spirit of power, and love, and self-control (2 Timothy 1:7).

Because, make no mistake: love and self-control require courage. Gregory the Great (540–604) said:

> *For the courage of the righteous is to subdue the flesh, to thwart our own wills, to annihilate the gratification of the present life, to be in love with the*

roughnesses of this world for the sake of eternal rewards, to set at nought the allurements of prosperity, to overcome the dread of adversity in our hearts.[3]

Do we have that courage, to fight valiantly those personal, intimate battles against the disordered desires of our own hearts, when the world and much of the church tells us we really needn't bother, and no-one would know or mind if we didn't?

In the rest of the Bible, being "strong and courageous" is often about doing what God has told you to do, trusting in his promise of help. Often with the reassurance of his comforting, strengthening presence, whether that's in conquering the land, building the temple, ending the exile or standing firm in the faith (see Numbers 13:20, Deuteronomy 31:6, 1 Chronicles 28:20, 2 Samuel 7:27, 10:12, and Isaiah 41:10). When Jesus is with us, we are strengthened. "It is I", he said, so "be of good courage!" (Matthew 14:27)

---

3 Gregory, *Moralia in Job*, Book 7.xxi (24).

We have no promises from the Lord of certain victory, in Synod debates and theological wranglings. We may lose. We may end up one day like the Episcopal Church in America – no separate province, no alternative oversight, the *Thirty-nine Articles* thrown on the bonfire. That may be the chastening the Lord has in mind for us. But as Augustine says "fortitude is love readily bearing all things for the sake of the loved object."[4] And we love the Church of England and God's people within it. We love the truth of the gospel. So we can resist the temptation to fight ecclesiastical battles with the weapons of this world; and take up instead the word of God and prayer, and the persuasive power of a godly life. "Whatever happens," says Paul, "conduct yourselves in a manner worthy of the gospel of Christ" (Philippians 1:27).

---

4 Augustine of Hippo, *On the Morals of the Catholic Church*, chapter 15.

Endurance in the face of setbacks

Being out of control and out of our comfort zones brings fear. There's been a lot of that in recent years. It's taken immense courage to do new types of ministry during the pandemic, that often involved tiring and steep learning curves. It's taken resolute determination to keep calm and carry on, taking difficult decisions, almost on a daily basis, which you know will upset or annoy at least some people in our congregations. Courage is unashamedly proclaiming the gospel together, whatever the cost.

And as we think of the arguments over *Prayers of Love and Faith*, I know many people are fearful of even mentioning the orthodox biblical view of marriage and sexuality in their churches. Of course we naturally want to shy away from bringing that up, when we already feel fragile and weak, or even traumatised, by the events of the last few years. Who needs more angst and argument right now? I don't.

In the last few years, I've personally been threatened by numerous individuals online with disciplinary proceedings, being reported to the police, threatened with violence, verbal and physical abuse, and even death, simply for having stood by the view of marriage and sexuality which I was asked to defend when I got ordained – which is the Church of England's official doctrine. I know many others have also faced flak too. You know the temptation to self-censorship can be immense.

So courage in our current situation is not about giving simple answers and then walking away, like a cocky student in an exam being asked what courage is. No. Courage is about endurance. As theologian Thomas Aquinas (1225-1274) puts it, "the principal act of fortitude is endurance, that is to stand immovable in the midst of dangers."[5]

But courage is *not* the same as foolhardiness, brawling and brashness. It is not, *nec-*

---

5 Thomas Aquinas, *Summa Theologiae* 2/2.123.6.

essarily, dramatic. But whatever it is, courage is not passive either, or incomplete – all talking and tweeting but never acting.

The other thing we have to say is that courage is not optional either. When I was crowdsourcing ideas on Facebook about courage (as one does these days), one person pointed out – rather startlingly I thought – that in Revelation 21:8, the first people listed as being thrown into hell (even before murderers, the sexually immoral, idolators and liars), are "the cowardly". The timid. The ones who run away.

Brothers and sisters, let that not be us. But rather, let us unashamedly proclaim the gospel together, whatever the cost in this life. Because we know there is a judgment day approaching.

That may mean speaking the truth that is hated by the world. It may also mean courageously confronting our own anxieties and inadequacies, our failures and our disunities. It's hard. But let's do it anyway, for the glory of God and the good of England.

Persistence

From Miletus, Paul sent to Ephesus for the elders of the church. When they arrived, he said to them: "You know how I lived the whole time I was with you, from the first day I came into the province of Asia. I served the Lord with great humility and with tears and in the midst of severe testing by the plots of my Jewish opponents. You know that I have not hesitated to preach anything that would be helpful to you but have taught you publicly and from house to house. I have declared to both Jews and Greeks that they must turn to God in repentance and have faith in our Lord Jesus.

"And now, compelled by the Spirit, I am going to Jerusalem, not knowing

what will happen to me there. I only know that in every city the Holy Spirit warns me that prison and hardships are facing me. However, I consider my life worth nothing to me; my only aim is to finish the race and complete the task the Lord Jesus has given me—the task of testifying to the good news of God's grace.

"Now I know that none of you among whom I have gone about preaching the kingdom will ever see me again. Therefore, I declare to you today that I am innocent of the blood of any of you. For I have not hesitated to proclaim to you the whole will of God. Keep watch over yourselves and all the flock of which the Holy Spirit has made you overseers. Be shepherds of the church of God, which he bought with his own blood. I know that after I leave, savage wolves will come in among you and will not spare the flock. Even from your own number men will arise and distort

the truth in order to draw away disciples after them. So be on your guard! Remember that for three years I never stopped warning each of you night and day with tears.

Now I commit you to God and to the word of his grace, which can build you up and give you an inheritance among all those who are sanctified. I have not coveted anyone's silver or gold or clothing. You yourselves know that these hands of mine have supplied my own needs and the needs of my companions. In everything I did, I showed you that by this kind of hard work we must help the weak, remembering the words the Lord Jesus himself said: 'It is more blessed to give than to receive.'"
(Acts 20:17-35 NIV)

There's a woman on X (formerly known as Twitter) who said a few years ago that her verse of the year was going to be 1 Kings 17:13. "Do not fear… but first, make me a little cake" (ESV). I think that's very inspiring. However, it may not be the best verse to start a new year, when many are thinking about slimming down or starting a new exercise regime. I think it may be better to go for Acts 20:24, from the passage above, which is my sporty daughter Cara's favourite verse. It says:

I consider my life worth nothing to me; my only aim is to finish the race and complete the task the Lord Jesus has given me—the task of testifying to the good news of God's grace.

We know that Paul did indeed complete his circuit. He says in 2 Timothy 4:7, using the same words, "I have fought the good fight, I have finished the race, I have kept the faith." Let's just think about how he did it – and about persistence in general – by looking at what he says here in Acts 20.

Persistence in duty

First, Paul says he ran his race openly, humbly, and with tears, in Acts 20:18 and 19. He was transparent about what he was doing and how it felt when it wasn't easy. Because it wasn't always easy. Yet he persisted.

He persisted because he had been given a race to run, a task to do. It wasn't just up to him to decide his own personal spiritual journey. He had been commissioned for a specific role by Christ. Just as many of us who are in ordained ministry, say, have made vows to undertake a particular task which is not ours to simply redefine at will as circumstances or our desires for individual spiritual expression change. If we confess that Jesus is our Lord, our Master, it is ours to discharge the duties of care he has given us, faithfully and determinedly.

Persistence despite opposition

Second, Paul ran against fierce opposition: particularly the "severe testing" and "plots" of his Jewish opponents which he mentions in Acts 20:19. That didn't stop him, however tempting it might have been on any number of occasions to simply let them have their way for the sake of a quieter life. He did not self-censor or cower away or give up in the face of difficulties and opposition. He persevered.

Persistence in teaching

Third, the apostle Paul ran his race by teaching clearly, in public and in private. Verse 20: "You know that I have not hesitated to preach anything that would be helpful to you but have taught you publicly and from house to house." He didn't, as some bishops seem to think they need to these days, choose silence in order to supposedly be a focus of unity for all. No, he did not hesitate (he says) to preach God's word in private, and even in public where it was much more dangerous.

God will have a lot to say to bishops, and indeed all Christians, who are very quick to tweet what they think about Brexit or the government, and yet pretend that silence on the church-defining issues of our day is anything but cowardice. They are what

John Calvin (1509-1564) calls "examples of inconstancy" or "monuments of instability".[6]

Paul did not hesitate to preach repentance and faith. But our temptation is to hedge our bets. Paul says again in verse 27 that he did not hesitate, to preach the whole will of God. Yet many today subordinate God's clearly expressed will to the devices and desires of their own hearts – and silently shrink back from affirming what God says. Let that not be us. Let us be unwearied and resolute in the race.

Persistence despite uncertainty

Fourthly, Paul continued running his race even when he couldn't see clearly what might happen. He says in verse 22 that he is compelled by the Spirit to go to Jerusalem. And he's going, even though he doesn't know what will happen to him there. He simply obeyed God, and left the outcomes to the Spirit. He knew there would be hard-

---

6 John Calvin, *Institutes of the Christian Religion*, 2.5.3.

ships ahead. There is no easy life anywhere: "in every place hardships await" he says. Yet he went ahead anyway, with dutiful diligence and conscientious constancy, because as he says elsewhere, "everyone who wants to live a godly life in Christ Jesus will be persecuted" (1 Timothy 3:12).

Some vicars have said to me that they don't know if they will be in their vicarages by the end of this year, because of where the bishops seem to be leading us in the Church of England. One can easily see why. It really should be more shocking to us that there is so much support for abandoning the Christian faith that was handed down to us and which our bishops promised to uphold. It says in our constitution,

> *The Church hath power to decree Rites or Ceremonies, and authority in Controversies of Faith: and yet it is not lawful for the Church to ordain any thing that is contrary to God's Word written, neither may it so expound one place of Scripture, that it be repugnant to an-*

other (Article 20).

And yet many bishops, clergy, and people in the Church are divisively pushing to do exactly what this says not to, plunging us into a damaging civil war. The persistent uncertainty that has resulted in recent years has been crippling, and sapping.

But let's not be dispirited. Let's be as steady as Paul was in the face of his uncertainties. As he says elsewhere, "as servants of God we commend ourselves in every way: *in great endurance*; in troubles, hardships and distresses" (2 Corinthians 6:4). Others may wander from the faith, but we are to pursue endurance (2 Timothy 6:10-11). We need to keep our heads, be sober-minded, or "keep calm and carry on".

Persistence in vigilance

Fifthly, Paul gave constant thought to his succession. He had taught these other elders and trained them up. He urges them now to keep watch over themselves, and also over the flock. He is insistent that they watch themselves, watch each other, because of verse 29:

> I know that after I leave, savage wolves will come in among you and will not spare the flock. Even from your own number men will arise and distort the truth in order to draw away disciples after them. So be on your guard! Remember that for three years I never stopped warning each of you night and day with tears.

Paul seems to have seen this coming. He knew that false teaching would arise, even amongst those he had himself trained up. He had warned them about this for three years – night and day – with urgency and emotion. He did everything he could to prevent heresy and apostasy and schism. He didn't plan for it so good disagreement could happen in an orderly way and they could all keep walking and working together despite their differences. No, he pleaded with them about false teaching and went on and on about it. It was that important. Woe to us if we think it can all be sorted nicely with a gentleman's agreement behind closed doors in comfortable smoke-free rooms so we don't have to worry about it.

Persistence for the prize

Sixth, Paul didn't run his race for money. He coveted no silver or gold or fine clothing — a mitre, a chasuble, a doctor's gown. The only inheritance he cared about was the ultimate prize — his inheritance among those who are being sanctified, which God's word of grace points us to. Ministry wasn't a living. It wasn't just his profession and a way to make a comfortable life. Apostolic ministry is focused on a future inheritance beyond the reach of the Church of England Clergy Pension scheme.

That's why he is eager to say in his farewell speech to the Ephesian elders that he is innocent of the blood of any of them. He had his eyes on a future day when he would be held accountable by God for everything he had said and done — especially for how he had carried out his ministry. He was running his race for a heavenly reward, and didn't want to lose it.

It was his job to save people from judgment and hell on that day, by warning them. As the *Book of Common Prayer* says, ministers are "messengers, watchmen, and stewards". If we fail to warn people, they will still be judged, and we along with them for our failure to tell them of the repentance and faith which could have saved them on that day. Paul is alluding in Acts 20:26 to Ezekiel 3 where the prophet is told to go to the people and tell them, "'This is what the Sovereign Lord says', whether they listen or fail to listen" (Ezekiel 3:10). He is then told that as a watchman, he will be accountable for the blood of those he does not warn to turn from their sin (Ezekiel 3:16-21).

But Paul has been clear and bold, and so is innocent of their blood. Can we be equally clear that we have spoken and taught with such openness and clarity about spiritual things, that we will escape condemnation too? Paul said, "I have declared to both Jews and Greeks that they must turn to God in repentance and have faith in our Lord Jesus" (Acts 20:21). Repentance, turning from sin and turning to God, has always been the essence of the message which watchmen are to proclaim. We are not here to affirm people in their sins or provide them with safe spaces in which to practice them. There is no safe space from the judgment of God. Except in Christ.

Persistence to the end

So, to conclude, think again of Acts 20:24.

> *I consider my life worth nothing to me; my only aim is to finish the race and complete the task the Lord Jesus has given me—the task of testifying to the good news of God's grace.*

This isn't a verse about living a comfortable life in the here and now. It is a verse about finishing the task we have been given in this world, so that we can enjoy the next. Our task, like Paul's, is to testify to the good news of God's grace in our generation, so that everyone can turn from their sin and live.

We haven't finished that task yet, and there is much still to be done. I've heard people say it is "game over" in the Church of England. But it is not game over. The game is still afoot. We may all sometimes be timid or slow in doing what needs to be done. But as Charles Spurgeon (1834–1892) preached:

> If in the heat of battle, when your helmet is bruised by some powerful enemy, you can still hold up your head, and say, "I know whom I have believed," and do not swerve from your post, then you are verily a child of heaven; for constancy, endurance, and perseverance, are the true marks of a hero of the cross, and of the invincible warriors of the Lord.[7]

---

7 C. H. Spurgeon, "A Bottle in the Smoke," in *The New Park Street Pulpit Sermons* (London: Passmore & Alabaster, 1856), 144.

Do you want to be "a hero of the cross", an "invincible warrior of the Lord"? Then do not swerve or swoon. Persist.

When Paul finished talking to the Ephesian elders in Acts 20, they did go on to have troubles, with a group called the Nicolaitans. But they withstood their heresies. So that Jesus himself wrote this to them, in Revelation 2:

> I know your deeds, your hard work and your perseverance. I know that you cannot tolerate wicked people, that you have tested those who claim to be apostles but are not, and have found them false. You have persevered and have endured hardships for my name, and have not grown weary. (Revelation 2:2-3).

His promise to them was "To the one who is victorious, I will give the right to eat from the tree of life, which is in the paradise of God" (Revelation 2:7). That is the promise for us, if we too can be right and persist.

As Augustus Toplady sang:

> *Tho' Satan, earth and self oppose,*
>
> *Yet, thro' thy help, I'll persevere;*
>
> *To Canaan's hills my eyes lift up,*
>
> *And choose my lot and portion there.*[8]

---

8 Augustus M. Toplady, *The Works of Augustus M. Toplady* (London; Edinburgh: William Baynes and Son; H. S. Baynes, 1825), 390.

Joy

Being in the Church of England right now can have a detrimental effect on one's mental health. I don't know about you, but I often find it exhausting and upsetting to read the latest news from the bishops or from General Synod. I open the *Church Times* each week and sigh, "O, joy … more disheartening news." I tried to give it up for Lent once, because it just wasn't doing me any good. But someone has to read it.

The Church of England can be seriously depressing. When one feels that the Bible is being sidelined and heresy is given free rein by those entrusted with spiritual safeguarding, while so many struggle to live life without Jesus in a spiritually needy nation; when there is institutional gaslighting, abuse of power by bishops, safeguarding nightmares, church decline, merging of parishes, theological squabbles, social media spats, the ghettoisation caused by the so-called Five Guiding Principles… it can all take its toll.

How can we cope with it all? What is the solution?

> *Do not be grieved, for the joy of the LORD is your strength.*
>
> *– Nehemiah 8:10.*

When emotions are wrong

At the time this verse was written, Ezra had just read the Old Testament law to the people from a wooden pulpit in Jerusalem. The Levites helped the people understand it clearly, expounding and applying it. This is a great high point in Israel's return from exile.

And what did the people do? They wept. They cried because they suddenly realised how far short of God's law they had fallen. They realised they were a long way from the glory days of David's victories and Solomon's Temple. They realised things were not as they should be, with them.

And what did Ezra and Nehemiah do? They told them to *stop* mourning and weeping. Seems wrong somehow, doesn't it? Surely they should have been content to see the people so affected by the reading of God's word. Surely they ought to have been glad that the message had hit home and was deeply impacting people. The word of God was doing its convicting work.

But the spiritual leaders of Israel told them they were having the wrong reaction. Their emotions were leading them to a false conclusion about the significance of what was happening. It wasn't a day for lamentation but for rejoicing. Because the Old Testament read to them was not only written to show them their sin, but also to remind them of God's covenant grace and favour towards them. So as Matthew Henry (1662-1714) says on this verse, "Even sorrow for sin must not grow so excessive as to hinder our joy in God and our cheerfulness in his service."[9] Don't cry, for the joy of the Lord is your strength.

What is this joy?

What kind of thing is this "joy"? It's not a carnal sensual joy, but a holy and spiritual thing — the joy *of the Lord*. It rejoices in the goodness of God and his government of the world and the church, as well as our own personal relationship with him. It makes us strong in his service; as Matthew Henry puts it, "Holy joy will be oil to the wheels of our obedience." And joy will also, he says,

> *... arm us against the assaults of our spiritual enemies, and put our mouths out of taste for those pleasures with*

---

9 Matthew Henry, *Matthew Henry's Commentary on the Whole Bible: Complete and Unabridged in One Volume* (Peabody: Hendrickson, 1994), 635.

which the tempter baits his hooks.[10]

Naturally, as part of the fruit of the Spirit (Galatians 5:22-23), joy protects us from the devil and his plots.

This is the kind of strength I need right now, after the conflicts we have had recently in the Church of England – a joy which empowers and lifts me up, even when I'm feeling rotten because of the circumstances in my life (or the serotonin in my brain). It may not change those things necessarily, but it certainly changes my soul, and my response to what is happening.

The effect of joy

When Charles Simeon (1759-1836) commented on this verse in Nehemiah, he pointed out various effects which joy in the Lord can have. First, it disposes us for action. "Fear and sorrow depress and overwhelm the soul", he said, and "they keep us from attending to any encouraging con-

---
10 Henry, *Matthew Henry's Commentary*, 635.

siderations." Every silver lining has a cloud when you're down; but look at it the other way around! Misery can make us neglect our immediate duties, and "We cannot pray, or speak, or do any thing with pleasure. On the contrary, a joyous frame exhilarates the soul."[11] As Proverbs 17:22 says, "A joyful heart is good medicine, but a crushed spirit dries up the bones."

Second, joy qualifies our suffering. When our spirits are oppressed, "we are apt to fret and murmur both against God and man," says Simeon. "We consider our trials as the effects of divine *wrath*; or, overlooking God, we vent our indignation against the instruments he uses." That is the wrong reaction. But on the other hand, Simeon says, "when the soul is joyous, afflictions appear light." Christians can rejoice if we are counted worthy of suffering for Christ and his word (Hebrews 10:34) and even sing in our prisons (Acts 16:25), and like Paul be "sorrowful,

---

11 Charles Simeon, *Horae Homileticae: Chronicles to Job* (London: Samuel Holdsworth, 1836), 295.

yet always rejoicing" (2 Corinthians 6:10).

"Let us not be always brooding over our corruptions", says Simeon — corruptions in ourselves, or in our church, I suppose. "Seasonable sorrows ought not to be discouraged" — there is a time and a place for lamentation (Friday morning, when you open the *Church Times* perhaps). But, adds the Cambridge evangelical pastor, "we should never lose sight of all that God has done for us. It is our privilege to walk joyfully before the Lord. If we abounded more in praise, we should more frequently be crowned with victory."

God's joy

When many people today think of God, they think of him either as a benevolent grandfatherly figure who smiles benignly at everything we do, or as an angry ogre in the sky who likes nothing more than to smite people for no good reason and demands adoration from servile followers. But God himself tells us very clearly what brings him joy — God is a God who loves repentance. The parable of the Prodigal Son in Luke 15 shows us that. As American preacher R. C. Sproul put it, "Certainly this parable makes it clear that nothing is more pleasing to God than our sincere sorrowing over sin and turning from it."[12]

All the parables in Luke 15 are basically Jesus's answer to the grumbling Pharisees at the beginning of the chapter. "Now the tax collectors and sinners were all gathering around to hear Jesus. But the Pharisees and the teachers of the law muttered, 'This man welcomes sinners and eats with them'" (Luke 15:1-2). They're grumbling and complaining because Jesus associates with people they did not consider worthy.

But Jesus spends time with and welcomes the dregs of society, the untouchables, the outcasts. He did spend time with the religious leaders too – Luke's shows him meeting and eating with Pharisees as well (Luke 14:1). But he didn't *only* associate with them. These

---

12 R. C. Sproul, *Pleasing God: Discovering the Meaning and Importance of Sanctification* (2nd edition; Colorado Springs: David C. Cook, 2012), chapter 7.

people of ill repute, these less respectable people wanted to hear Jesus too. And the Pharisees didn't like it. It didn't seem right to them that this great teacher and prophet should mix with such people.

And to justify his policy of spending time with those who were labelled "sinners", Jesus tells three parables. The key points are the same in all three: God eagerly searches for people that are lost, and he celebrates with joy when he finds them.

So we see this in the parable of the lost sheep. The shepherd loses one sheep, so he leaves the ninety-nine and goes looking for the lost one. When he finds it, he is overjoyed. And Jesus concludes: "Just so, I tell you, there will be more joy in heaven over one sinner who repents than over ninety-nine righteous persons who need no repentance" (Luke 15:7). Joy in heaven! A party to celebrate the recovery of what was lost.

It's the same point in the parable of the lost coin. The woman loses one of her coins.

She looks high and low to find it. When she does, she's not only relieved. She's ecstatic. Luke 15:10: "Just so, I tell you, there is joy before the angels of God over one sinner who repents."

God is like the shepherd. God is like the woman. He eagerly searches for lost people – like these sinners and tax collectors – and celebrates when he finds them. He loves finding sinners. They are "found" when they repent. That is, we know God has found them when they turn back to him. God loves repentance – he loves finding people and saving them from being lost forever.

That's basically the message of the parable of the prodigal son too. Or rather, as it should perhaps be called, the parable of the forgiving Father. Because it's the Father who's the most important character in the story, not the prodigal son, that is, the son who runs away and squanders his father's wealth in wild living. We're meant to see the connection to the other two parables. God is the Father figure who rejoices at the repentance of his wayward son coming home. And we're meant to see his connection to the sinners and tax collectors – God loves that they're crowding round to hear Jesus. It means they're thinking of coming home.

God loves it when we repent and turn back to him instead of living life our own way. Speaking of what he calls "communion with God", the puritan John Owen (1616–1683) said, "It is the gladness of the heart of Christ, the joy of his soul, to take poor sinners into this relation with himself. He rejoiced in the thoughts of it from eternity, Proverbs 8:31; and always expresses the greatest willingness to undergo the hard task required for that."[13] That's why, "For the joy set before him he endured the cross, scorning its shame" (Hebrews 12:2). He did it gladly, for us and for our salvation.

---

13 John Owen, *The Works of John Owen* (ed. William H. Goold; Edinburgh: T&T Clark, 1850-53), 2:55. I have updated the language slightly.

Sharing God's joy

There's something else we should notice about these parables Jesus told. They are not just teaching us about God's love of our repentance. They are inviting us *to share it*. They are inviting us to rejoice with God.

Ponder a curious detail which is often missed in the first two parables in Luke 15. The shepherd finds his sheep and then rejoices. Is that what it says? Yes, but that's not all. Luke 15 verse 6: "Then he calls his friends and neighbours together and says, '*Rejoice with me*; I have found my lost sheep.'"

And then again in the second parable. The woman finds her coin, and she is glad. So then, verse 9 – "when she finds it, she calls her friends and neighbours together and says, '*Rejoice with me*; I have found my lost coin.'"

It seems a strange and unnecessary detail if the only message is that God loves repentance. In both cases there's something more. The figure that stands for God – the shepherd or the woman – invites friends and neighbours to join in the rejoicing. Because God's friends share God's delight in the recovery of the lost.

And the parable of the forgiving father is no different. The father had two sons. His second son was unhappy with the lavish welcome given to his wayward brother. Clearly if the prodigal son is a picture of the sinners and tax collectors flocking to hear Jesus, then this elder son is meant to be the Pharisees themselves. They've been grumbling about Jesus's warm welcome for those less respectable, less pious than themselves. Like the elder brother, they hear that God has received such people, and they are angry and refuse to join the party.

They don't love repentance. They love the status quo. They have a passion for devout respectability. They're quite happy to be the only ones enjoying privileged access to the father, and they don't really want to share it. And Jesus pictures God the Father coming out to plead with these Pharisaical older brothers. God implores them to be happy that the prodigal has come home, and that sinners are turning back to God. But they're not. They resent the extravagant attention being given to the newcomers. They grumble and complain because the father is so gracious and kind.

There are always two choices when we're confronted with God's grace. We can either join him in the party, rejoice in his generosity to those (including us) who don't deserve it, and go looking for other lost sheep whose recovery will gladden the heart of God. Or we can grumble. Say, "this church is for people like *us* not them. We don't want them dragging our good reputation down." Would we rather celebrate with our friends while our brothers rot in the pigsty — as they deserve — or will we be as compassionate as the father, and celebrate with him when our brother comes home?

It's a very unsatisfactory ending to the story. Because we don't know what the elder brother did. Did he swallow his pride, smile with his father and make up with his brother? Or did he stomp off in a huff? The reason Jesus doesn't tell us the ending is because he's inviting the Pharisees, and he's inviting us, to write the ending ourselves. He's inviting us to join the party, and bring joy to God's heart (and our own) by reaching out to those who are far off. Wherever they are. Whatever they have done.[14]

Where to find joy

It's surprising how often the Bible talks about joy specifically in difficult contexts. Peter wrote to suffering churches, and yet he said since they believed in Jesus they could "rejoice with joy that is inexpressible and filled with glory" (1 Peter 1:8). James, similarly, said "Count it all joy, my brothers, when you meet trials of various kinds" (James 1:2). The Thessalonians "received the word in much affliction, with the joy of the Holy Spirit" (1 Thessalonians 1:6), and

---

14 See Lee Gatiss, *Living to Please God* (London: IVP, 2024).

Paul told the Romans to "rejoice in hope, be patient in tribulation, be constant in prayer" (Romans 12:12). Joy assumes and almost seems to *need* trying circumstances, and flourishes within them!

Jesus set the path, of course; as the writer to the Hebrews tells us, we need to be "looking to Jesus, the founder and perfecter of our faith, who for the *joy* that was set before him endured the cross, despising the shame, and is seated at the right hand of the throne of God" (Hebrews 12:2). To find joy in confusing and demoralising times, we need to look to him. He alone "is able to keep you from stumbling and to present you blameless before the presence of his glory with great joy" (Jude 24).

God has given us his unerring word in order to bring us joy. John says "we are writing these things so that our joy may be complete" (1 John 1:4). And he has given us his people as a source of joy too: "I have no greater joy than to hear that my children are walking in the truth" (3 John 4). So these are things to focus on if we wish to obey Paul's command to "rejoice in the Lord; again I will say, rejoice" (Philippians 4:2). Read his word, meet his faithful people, focus on what the Lord has done for us.

So if you, like me, feel less than sanguine about the situation we are in right now in the Church of England, we need to challenge our internal monologues and remind ourselves to rejoice in the Lord. For that is our true strength. As Martin Lloyd-Jones said in his book *Spiritual Depression*, "Have you realized that most of your unhappiness in life is due to the fact that you are listening to yourself instead of talking to yourself?"[15] If you are downcast or in turmoil like the Psalmist (Psalm 42:5), give yourself a good talking to, as he does. Do not rejoice in wrongdoing, but rejoice with the truth (1 Corinthians 13:6).

And so let us pray for one another, with Paul:

---

15 D. Martyn Lloyd-Jones, *Spiritual Depression: Its Causes and Cures* (London: Pickering and Inglis, 1965), 20.

May the God of hope fill you with all joy and peace in believing, so that by the power of the Holy Spirit you may abound in hope" (Romans 15:13).

We may not be optimistic about the Church of England at the moment, but we can always be full of joy and hope in our Lord and Saviour, Jesus Christ. So may he strengthen us with all power "according to his glorious might, for all endurance and patience with joy" (Colossians 1:11). We are going to need it.

Gospel Flourishing in a Time of Confusion

This book addresses key questions facing Anglican Evangelicals at this moment of confusion and uncertainty. Should we stay in the Church of England, and make use of the many gospel opportunities it affords? Or should we leave for pastures new, since things within the established church have become so difficult? What does it mean to be a "righteous remnant" in an apostate church, when everyone seems to be doing "what is right in their own eyes"? And are there lessons we can learn from how our ancestors handled these sorts of questions, not just in recent times but in the very earliest days of the church?

Five bishops, pastors, and theologians offer here a resource to help us think through the issues, that the gospel of Jesus might flourish and spread in our nation.

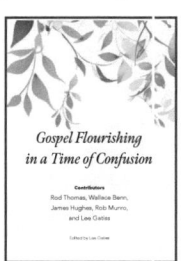

www.churchsociety.org * admin@churchsociety.org

FIGHT VALIANTLY

What does it mean "to contend for the faith that was once for all delivered to the saints"? With so much confusion and argument in today's church, how are Christians meant to think about and react to false teaching? How can we promote the gospel lovingly in a context of opposition?

"We don't like contending, but sometimes faithfulness to Christ requires that we must. This book helpfully takes us to the Bible to show us why and how. An excellent resource for individuals, PCC members, and whole churches."

> Vaughan Roberts, Rector of St Ebbe's Oxford

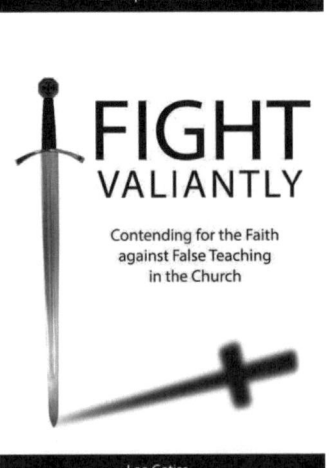

Available from Church Society
www.churchsociety.org
admin@churchsociety.org

PB, 292 pages
ISBN: 9781739937645

WALK *this* WAY

Guided reflections on Christian faith, life, and prayer for individuals and groups

For many centuries, people have learned what it means to be a Christian through the Apostles' Creed, the Ten Commandments, and the Lord's Prayer. Billions of people have been baptised into the faith, regularly attended church, and celebrated the Lord's Supper, but they haven't always understood what they are all about. If you need help to really get going or inspiration to continue on your own journey as a Christian, this book is for you. It takes a careful look at those major signposts along the way, and lights the path ahead with clarity and grace.

"This excellent book will help establish new believers in the faith, refresh longstanding saints in the truths of God's Word, guide those who are being trained for various ministries in the church and be a valuable resource for clergy and other leaders who are training them."

Andrew Cheah,
Dean of St Mary's Cathedral, Kuala Lumpur

www.churchsociety.org * admin@churchsociety.org

offering strategic leadership

For more than 180 years, Church Society has been contending to reform and renew the Church of England in biblical faith, on the basis of its Reformed foundations as expressed in the doctrine of the Articles, the worship of the Prayer Book, and the ministry of the Ordinal.

Church Society

EQUIPPING GOD'S
PEOPLE TO LIVE
GOD'S WORD

To find out more and to join Church Society, please visit our website, churchsociety.org

  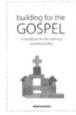

resourcing today's church

Church Society publishes several new books each year, bringing the best of our Anglican Evangelical heritage to new generations, and responding to new pressures and opportunities in today's Church and nation. We also produce a weekly podcast, a quarterly magazine and a theological journal, as well as our regular blog.

serving tomorrow's church

As part of our commitment to raising up a new generation of leaders, we host the annual Junior Anglican Evangelical Conference for those in the early stages of ministry. Church Society also has patronage of around 130 parishes, helping to protect evangelical ministry in the Church of England for the future.